The Ori
Develop

Roman L
Vestments

Raymund James

From the Brass of
Thos. Nelond, in
Cowfold Church,
Sussex (1433)

St. Thomas of Canterbury

Roman Catholic Books
Post Office Box 2286, Fort Collins, CO 80522
booksforcatholics.com

"All that promotes the glory of God, the dignity of the sacred rites, and the solemn splendour of divine worship, is justly the object of Our approval and encouragement."

From the Bull of our Holy Father Pius XI, dated Ascension Day, 1933, appointing H.E.Cardinal McRory his Legate for the ceremony of laying the Foundation Stone of Liverpool Cathedral.

ISBN 978-1-929291-25-0

Anderson] [*Rome*

FIGURE I.

EFFIGY OF POPE MARTIN V.

(✠ 1431)

In the Confession of the Lateran Basilica.

Felici] [*Rome*

FIGURE II.

HIS HOLINESS POPE PIUS XI SAYING MASS IN ST. PETER'S ON ST. JOSEPH'S DAY, MARCH 19TH, 1930.

He is wearing the chasuble made for him by the Poor Clares of Mazamet in France, and an alb with a continuous embroidered apparel round the skirt. The chasuble is cut approximately to the shape numbered IX in the diagram at the end of this book, and is enriched with a Y-cross. The assistant prelates wear the surplice over the rochet ; hence the double flounce of lace, one flounce belonging to each vestment. The linen of these vestments is heavily starched and crimped into minute zig-zag pleats ; that of the Holy Father's alb is of course ironed out flat.

FIG. III.

CHASUBLE CUT ON THE LINES OF THOSE OF THE XII AND XIII CENTURIES (No. I in Diagram).

The stand is about the height of the shoulders of a man 6 feet tall.

THE ORIGIN & DEVELOPMENT OF ROMAN LITURGICAL VESTMENTS

By Raymund James

AS there seems to be a most welcome tendency nowadays on the part of Catholics to return once more to an appreciation and love of that form of public worship and prayer which is so essentially the Church's own—we mean the Sacred Liturgy—it may not be without interest to set down briefly a few notes on the origin, history, and development of those vestments which in the course of time have become inseparable from the rites and ceremonies of the Western Church, and which are now ordinarily worn by the ministers of the altar and seen by every Catholic whenever he attends the liturgical functions of the Church.

In the liturgy of the earliest Christian centuries no special vestments were employed, just as no special language was used therein; it was performed by the clergy in their ordinary clothes—probably in their best clothes at first, and subsequently in garments still of everyday form, but specially set apart for use at the altar. Hence first arose the idea of special liturgical vestments, and it was only little by little that, as the secular fashions changed, the official vestments, whose form hardly altered at all, became distinct and different from the ordinary civilian dress. Thus, from time to time we notice various councils and synods adjusting the use of the different garments, and drawing little by little a clearer line between lay attire and that of the altar, and even between the dress of clerics when engaged in the liturgy and their raiment at other times. Thus we find, for example, St. Boniface in the VIIIth century ordering his priests and deacons to wear *chasubles* for the liturgy and not ordinary civilian clothes.[1] Two centuries earlier, St. Cesarius of Arles had had a "*casula villosa*" for ordinary wear, and another one which he was accustomed to use in processions.[2] In this matter St. Fulgentius of Ruspe seems to have been somewhat

[1] Cabrol, *Dictionnaire d'Archéologie Chrétienne et de Liturgie*, T. III—I, col. 1191.

[2] *Vita S. Caes. Arelat*, I, No. 32, Migne, *P.L.* LXVII, col. 1017; *Testamentum S. Caes. Arelat, ibid.* col. 1140; Cabrol, *op. cit.*, col. 1183, 1190, 1191, 1193.

conservative, for after the custom was established of keeping at least a special tunic or alb for use at the altar, he continued to use for Mass the one he wore at other times and even at night, saying that one should " change one's heart " on approaching the altar " and not one's raiment."[1] Even as late as the end of the IXth century this same practice had to be expressly forbidden by Bishop Riculph in the diocese of Soissons.[2]

As a result of this gradual development of special vestments from the ordinary garb of the day, we shall naturally expect to find that all the chief civil garments of the Ist and IInd centuries of our era will have left their mark upon the liturgical vestments of later ages; and this is indeed the case, as we shall see, with the one notable exception of the toga, which, being the distinctive garb of those only who were legally Roman citizens, was therefore out of reach of many of the early Christian laity and clergy. In its place was worn *a large garment of conical form*, reaching practically to the feet all round, and with a hole, either square, round or oblong, at the apex, for the head. The hands were freed by bunching up the material at the sides on to the arms. This garment was sometimes substituted for the toga even by those who had a right to the latter and, as time went on, officials of the state began to wear it even on public occasions. It thus received a character of importance and solemnity, and was very naturally chosen as the most proper garment for priests engaged in offering the August Sacrifice. It was known variously as the *pænula* or *phenolium*, the *amphibalum*—this name implying the enveloping character of the garment—the *planeta* or the *casula*. The origin of the word *planeta* is obscure, but the most probable derivation is that from the root of *planare*, " to wander," and thus the name refers to a garment which was worn out of doors and on journeys; it is no doubt for this reason that we see Mercury symbolically attired in it. This has always been, and still is, the ordinary name for the chasuble in Rome, while *casula* has from the earliest times been its common appellation in the Provinces. The word *casula* is correctly considered by St. Isidore of Seville to be a diminutive of *casa*, a house, and so to mean a " little house " or " tent." " *Casula*," he says,[3] " *est vestis cucullata, dicta per diminutionem a casa, quod*

1 *AA.SS. Bol.* Jan. I. p. 39; Cabrol, *op. cit.* col. 1191, 1199.
2 *Constitutio Riculfi*, VII, (A.D. 889); Labbé, *Concilia*, IX, col. 418 (Paris, 1671).
3 *De Orig.*, XIX, xxi; *P.L.*, LXXXII, col. 691.

totum hominem tegat, quasi minor casa. Unde et cuculla quasi minor cella." From this we may note that St. Isidore regards the chasuble as hooded. Undoubtedly many, though by no means all, of the early ones had a hood attached. Evidences of this hood survive to-day in the cope (of which more anon) and in the monastic scapular, in connexion with which it is interesting to note that while the chasuble, through reverence for its sacred use, retained for over a thousand years its original ample and quasi-conical form in the Liturgy, in ordinary life it became little by little so clipped at the sides that by the XIIth century it had assumed the form of the present hooded scapular ; and though this continued to be made of the original material, namely, wool, the Mass-chasuble, again through reverence, had by that time been almost everywhere turned into a garment of silk.

While its sacred use in the Liturgy rendered the chasuble at this period immune from mutilation, some means had to be found for giving the celebrant and his assistants more play for their arms. In the case of the celebrant, this was done by the assistance of the deacons, who lifted up the sides of his chasuble whenever necessary. Hence, clearly, originated that custom of the Roman Rite in virtue of which the deacon and subdeacon lift up the celebrant's chasuble at the incensation of the altar ; and here it is worth noting that, according to Martinucci[1], the ministers should not let go the chasuble once it has been raised, even when genuflecting, until the incensation is quite finished ; this practice can only have originated at a time when the chasuble was so wide and steep-sided that it would have been inconvenient to have let it go while the thurible was yet in the celebrant's hands. The similar direction to the deacon or server to raise the chasuble at the Elevation[2] is clearly also the outcome of the use of ample and steep-sided chasubles, with which alone such assistance is really necessary. With the diminutive clipped chasubles now unfortunately all too common, which are already cut away right up to the shoulders, or with wider but high-sided ones, such help is altogether superfluous.

Now, the deacons had no one to lift up their chasubles for them, so, before approaching the sanctuary, they folded them up and secured them in such a way as to give themselves the required freedom—very much as nowadays we roll up our sleeves

[1] *Lib.* I, *Vol.* I, c. xiii, § 1, No. 18 (Rome 1879).
[2] Miss. Rom. *Rit. Cel.*, VIII, 6, 8.

before beginning manual work. There is indeed a fresco in one of the Catacombs of about 300 A.D. shewing a soldier with the sides of his *pænula* thus rolled up. This is clearly the origin of our folded chasuble of to-day, as worn by deacon and sub-deacon in penitential seasons, the only reason why the front is now folded instead of the sides being that so often there are no longer any sides left to fold. A further device for obtaining freedom of movement was to remove the chasuble altogether, roll it up and place it over the shoulder, securing the ends with the girdle; this was the origin of the present "broad stole," which has developed as a separate vestment out of the practical impossibility of any longer folding up the chasuble on account of its stiffness and diminutive size. The original method is, we believe, still sometimes followed, and is actually given as the normal one in the Roman Missal[1], the "broad stole" being mentioned as a substitute only.

The conical form of the early chasuble was constant all over the Roman Empire. We have seen what St. Isidore of Seville had to say about it; another early writer thus described it :[2] "The *casula*, also known as the *amphibalum*, which the priest wears, is all joined together. . . . It is without sleeves, for the priest blesses" (*i.e.*, prays, consecrates) "rather than ministers" (an allusion to the difficulty of working with the arms in a chasuble). "Hence it is *joined together all round, not divided, nor open*; for many are the hidden mysteries of sacred Scripture which the learned priest should keep hidden as beneath a seal, and he should moreover keep the unity and not fall away into heresy and schism." Rabanus Maurus (IXth cent.) identifies the *planeta* and the *casula* in his definition[3] : "The priest's '*planeta*' is commonly called the '*casula*,' for it *covers him up like a small house*; it is the topmost of all his vestments, and it covers up and protects all the other ones that are underneath it."

The material of the early chasuble was generally wool, silk being as yet uncommon in the West, and its colour varied; but if we can trust pictorial representations, each chasuble was of a simple colour without mixture or pattern, and vestments seem frequently to have been unlined. Soon, however, garments

[1] Miss Rom. *Rub. Gen*, XIX, 6.

[2] *Apud* Martène, *Thes. Anecdot.* V, where it is ascribed to St. Germanus of Paris (VIth cent.)—cfr. Cabrol, *op. cit.*, col. 1175. Marriott, *Vestiarium Christianum*, Appendix D, p. 204, gives it a later date and points out that as St. Germanus is *quoted* in it he cannot well have written it himself.

[3] *De Instit. Clericorum*, I, 21.

which were definitely set aside for liturgical use, and specially chasubles intended for the use of the bishop or other celebrant, shewed a tendency to become very rich and even sumptuous. Thus, to give but one example, St. Augustine of Canterbury is recorded to have sent his friend St. Livin as an ordination present, a "*casula purpurea auro gemmisque composite ornata,*" and a "*stola cum orario*" (this probably means simply a stole) "*gemmis pretiosis auroque fulgido pertexta.*"[1] At first white, being the ordinary Roman festal colour, was generally used for important feasts, and especially at Easter-tide, and black or a dark colour for the penitential seasons and days.

Very important, too, in its bearing on later developments, is the construction of the early chasuble, for even in the darkest days of the XVIIIth century the old traditional forms were not completely abandoned, though the vestment makers of those times did their best to render them quite unrecognisable; and even in our own day, when some serious and widespread efforts are being made to restore once more the beauty of God's House in accordance with the true Christian tradition, the high standard of much otherwise fine work is unfortunately lowered by its being grounded so much more on enthusiasm for, than on a critical knowledge of, this tradition. And nowhere is this truer than in the case of the sacred vestments, and in particular of the chasuble. In the *Dictionnaire d'Archéologie Chrétienne et de Liturgie*, for example, the learned writer of the articles on the cope and the chasuble states that the original *casula* or *planeta* was a flat circular garment with a hole for the head in the centre, but this is not in accordance with facts, nor is it borne out even by the illustrations which accompany the articles themselves. As the result of our own researches at home and abroad, and indeed from a study of the illustrations in the *Dictionnaire* itself, we have no hesitation in affirming, with Braun and others, that the original chasuble was, as we have said before, a *conical* garment, and not a flat circle of material. It was made out of a more or less semi-circular piece of stuff, like a cope, brought round at the sides, and sewn together right down the front, leaving an opening at the apex for the head to pass through. Owing to the exigencies of the material, sometimes two pieces or more would be used, one or more for each side, thus necessitating a similar seam down the middle of the back; but these

[1] *Vita S. Livini, apud* Rock, *Church of our Fathers* (1st edn.) Vol. I, p. 357, note 11; or Mabillon, *AA.SS.B.*, II, p. 436.

two or more pieces were never used as front and back, so as to produce seams down the shoulders and arms. This conical form, then, was undoubtedly the form which is illustrated in all the old frescoes and mosaics and illuminations, and indeed, actually exemplified by the oldest chasubles still in existence, as, for example, the so-called chasuble of St. Régnobert at Bayeux, dating from the XIth century, those of St. Thomas of Canterbury at Sens and Tournai, one in the cathedral of Würzburg, and several others, illustrations of some of which will be found in Braun (*I Paramenti Sacri*) and Rock (*Church of our Fathers*, Vol. I); one said to have belonged to St. Bernard is illustrated in the *Catholic Encyclopedia* s.v. Bernard. The average radius of these ancient chasubles, which, since they were made from a rough semi-circle of material, is more or less constant throughout, is about 60 inches, and their perimeter is from 5 to 5½ yards. The few modern conical chasubles which we have seen or ourselves made reproduce faithfully the folds and general conformation of those of the medieval or earlier periods which are pictured for us in MSS., stained glass, brasses, or in monuments of stone, while the flat circular or oval chasubles which have come under our notice have not produced the same results at all, but have hung and draped themselves in a totally different and quite untraditional manner.

Before long it became the general custom to cover the principal seams back and front, and to bind the neck aperture and hem with bands or strips of material whose original object was the entirely practical one of hiding and strengthening the seams, but which soon became an ornamental feature as well. Their symbolic meaning, together with most other symbolism, was of a later date, though finally it entirely supplanted the earlier utilitarian motive, and turned these bands, which from their rich character were called *auriphrygia* or " orphreys," into mere adornments.

We may now pass on to the Cope. Chasubles, as we have already said, were of two varieties: hooded and without hood. Now, the hood was appended to the chasuble not for mere ornament's sake, but to be used, and generally speaking such hooded chasubles were employed for outdoor processions—note the name *pluviale* or " rainproof "—and were worn also in quire and on ceremonial occasions by many or all the assistant clergy or brethren. Obviously the chasuble, from its very form, militated against the comfort of a cleric who had to carry, say, a reliquary, in a long procession, and after a time it became necessary to find some means of relief. We have seen how in the case of the unhooded chasuble—the sacrificial garment—any idea of cutting, or even any extensive clipping operations, would have been considered almost sacrilegious at this time: for the chasuble was essentially a garment "uncut, closed-in on all sides," and already had its mystical significance as such; but in the case of the processional garment, and that used for quire and for ceremonies other than the Mass, the same hesitancy was evidently not felt, for at a very early date the idea seems to have occurred to people to leave the front seam (often even in sacrificial chasubles open for a few inches at the bottom) either unsewn to a point about half-way up, or entirely open, in which latter case the garment was secured by a clasp, called the "morse," thus producing a vestment almost identical in shape and appearance with the cope as we know it now. The original copes, like the original chasubles, were in all probability of wool, not unlike the Dominican *cappa*. It became gradually the custom on feast-days to use silk copes instead of the woollen ones, and the silk cope seems to have become amongst other things one of the special privileges of cantors. It is from these silk quire or ceremonial copes that we have derived on the one hand the *cappa magna*, and on the other the modern liturgical cope.

What we now know as the Alb, was originally called the *tunica manicata alba*—the white tunic with sleeves—and was essentially not a topmost garment, though a considerable amount of it was often exposed to view. It frequently had a band of enrichment right round the cuffs and the hem of the skirt, though, when the dalmatic was worn over it, this latter garment often appropriated the rich band, leaving the alb altogether plain and unadorned. All the early and medieval albs were of full length reaching quite down to the ground, whence this garment was also called the *tunica talaris*. In this connexion we may note, even now, the rubric[1] which directs the celebrant and his minister between them to *raise* and arrange the alb over the girdle when vesting, and the practice of still further lifting up its hem as the celebrant ascends the altar steps.

The *tunica Dalmatica* was a form of tunic, or as we should

[1] Missale Rom., *Rit. Cel.*, I, 3.

now say, a sort of alb, originally made of Dalmatian wool, and differentiated from an ordinary alb, at first, principally by the width and fulness of the sleeves, which were not unlike those of a modern surplice and reached to the wrists, and by the fact that it was worn ungirt. It was originally introduced into Rome in imperial times as an exotic fashion, and seems never to have supplanted the *tunica talaris*, or alb, but to have been worn over it, in addition to or even in place of the outer cloak or mantle, and to have been generally a few inches shorter than it. Like the very early albs, it was almost always, though not universally, enriched with vertical stripes, called *clavi*, extending from shoulders to feet, back and front ; these were of a bright red, russet or purple colour—that known as *purpureum*. Round the sleeve, a little way from the hem, was a similar stripe, and, at the hem, as also round the bottom edge of the body, was often a band of rich ornament ; these enrichments, which were virtually the same as those of the alb, were the forerunners of the medieval apparels. The dalmatic had been adopted for deacons in Rome as early as the IVth century, when the Pope also took to wearing one, and eventually two, under his chasuble ; later this practice was extended to deacons and bishops in other parts of Christendom. As it was a festal garment, however, deacons did not use it on penitential occasions, but at such times continued, as they do still, to wear the chasuble. The use of the dalmatic was subsequently extended, as the result of not a little agitation, to sub-deacons ; but their tunicle at first was a dalmatic in form only, and shorn of most of its ornament. Throughout the Middle Ages the dalmatic continued to be a very long and graceful garment, reaching well below the knees, and with sleeves long enough at least to cover the elbows. With regard to the development of its ornament, we shall examine this briefly when speaking of apparels.

A word or two on the origin of the stole and maniple will be of interest. The former at first was nothing more than a sort of face-towel—the original name *orarium* (from *os*, *oris*) meaning simply this, and having nothing to do with the word *orare*, "to pray." It was worn by deacons over the left shoulder, hanging down back and front over the dalmatic, ready for immediate use ; though from the first it may have fulfilled a ceremonial rather than a practical role, and in any case it soon became a mere appendage, and was looped on the right thigh to prevent it flapping about and slipping off, and finally, by the VIIIth century in Rome, it was worn under the dalmatic instead of over it. Clerks in minor orders and sub-deacons made an unsuccessful bid for the use of the stole at about this time. From an expression used by the Fourth Council of Toledo[1] in 633, the stole (*orarium*) appears to have been by that time common to deacons, priests, and bishops in Spain, and the council held at Braga in 675[2] ordered the priest to wear the stole round his neck and crossed upon his breast, as is done to-day.

St. Fulgentius, true to his principles, consistently refused to wear the *orarium* in imitation of other bishops—though it is only fair to say that this probably referred to ordinary and not to liturgical use.[3] Such extra-liturgical use of the stole in the Latin Church is now, so far as we know, confined to the Pope alone ; though in some places parish priests wear it in processions to distinguish them from the other clergy.

How the word *stola* came to be substituted for the older word *orarium* is not clear. Setting aside the various meanings of the Greek στολή, its Latin form *stola* as used by classical writers generally meant the large and ample robe worn by matrons, though this connotation was never very definite or exclusive. It came gradually to be applied to the liturgical *orarium* during the course of the VIIIth and IXth centuries in the provinces, where its meaning had probably become by that time quite indefinite, and after the original name had become less apt owing to the development of the vestment itself. This original name survived in Rome for perhaps another hundred years, but even there it finally gave way before its rival, and for many centuries now the word *stola* has been the only one in use throughout the Latin Church ; the word *orarium*, in its Greek form ὠράριον, has survived only as the name for the deacon's stole in the Oriental Rites.

The maniple started life as a napkin, a sort of large folded purificator, and was made of linen and carried in the hand. This, like the stole, may have had at first a practical use or may have been rather a ceremonial appendage, something after the manner of a modern waiter's napkin. A fine example of a linen maniple held in the hand occurs in a fresco in the church of

[1] *Conc. Tolet.*, IV, *c.* XL ; Labbé, *Concilia*, V, col. 1716.
[2] *Conc. Bracar.*, IV, *c.* IV ; Labbé, *Concilia*, VI, col. 564.
[3] *AA.SS. Bol.*, Jan. I, p. 39.

San Clemente in Rome. The maniple remained in this more or less practical state for many centuries after the stole had become a mere ornament, and traces of linen maniples are found as late as the twelfth century. A relic of the practical origin of the maniple is to be found in the custom of only wearing it at the altar itself, or in the ceremonies directly connected with the Mass, for here originally would be its only sphere of usefulness, in wiping the vessels and the celebrant's and ministers' hands or mouths. It was at first carried only by the priest and deacon, but was extended to sub-deacons in the XIth or XIIth century, when the sub-diaconate was reckoned as a major order, and of this order it is now the distinguishing mark ; attempts to extend its use to lower orders were put down by Authority.

Incidentally one may note how much more convenient is the old long maniple than the modern short one, since, while the latter is very liable to get on the altar and be in the way, the former hangs down in front of it and is never a nuisance or a danger.

The amice was almost the last of the present liturgical vestments to be adopted officially as such. Even to-day in many Eastern rites it is not an official vestment, though each minister may produce a neckcloth and fold it round his neck before vesting. The amice, again, like all the other vestments was in origin purely practical, and, like our modern collar, was devised to prevent the vestments from being soiled by the neck or hair. It became a prominent and important vestment only at a later date, when it was ornamented or apparelled with a rich collar, and was used also to cover the head until this function, except in the case of certain religious, was transferred to the biretta.

We have now arrived at the early medieval period, roughly from the IXth to the end of the XIIth century, which corresponds approximately to the great Romanesque period of building in Western Europe. So far, we have been chiefly concerned with the origin and early development of the various vestments adopted for liturgical use. At the time of which we are now speaking, these had become standardised in form, in use, in material, and to a great extent, though by no means altogether, in colour, throughout the Latin Church. One of the circumstances which greatly conduced to this standardisation of liturgical garments was the fact that by now the sacred vestments had become survivals of an otherwise extinct set of fashions, and found practically no counterpart in the garments of civil life; they had come to be recognised as definitely set apart for the use of the ministers employed in the liturgical services of the Church. Silk, too, had by this time become much more common in the West, and the desire, growing in proportion to the increasing importance of the Church, of surrounding the Divine Worship with as much splendour as possible, led to the employment of the finest silk and gold for the making of vestments, in place of the more workaday materials formerly used. Thus, by the end of the IXth century, the silk chasuble had become so common in Gaul that Riculph of Soissons could order his priests to use it to the exclusion of any other.[1] Inventories of this period, of which a number are still extant, give catalogues of many rich chasubles, copes, and other vestments, not a few adorned with jewels.[2] The finest of these would have far exceeded in beauty of workmanship and wealth of enrichment anything that we produce to-day. Generally the material of the vestments was plain and of a single colour, the embroidery and jewellery being confined to the orphreys, which at this time began to develop into a prominent ornamental feature, though ever retaining their usefulness in covering the seams and binding the edges of the vestments. Sometimes, however, the orphreys were altogether omitted, especially in the case of chasubles, and the whole vestment was covered with embroidery or powdered with jewels.

The great prevalence at this time of attaching mystical and symbolical meanings to everything used in connexion with the liturgy, was the cause of many treatises on this subject being written; and from these we may indirectly gather many valuable indications as to the shape of the liturgical vestments of the time. Thus, St. Bruno of Segni (late XIth century) says: "What is indicated by the *planeta* or *casula*, but charity? For this garment covers and contains within itself all the other vestments, just as in charity are contained all the commandments of the Law and the Prophets."[3] Rupert of Duyts (early XIIth century), a prolific writer on these matters, says: "The chasuble

[1] *loc. cit.*
[2] See several examples mentioned in Rock, *op. cit.*, p. 358, note.
[3] *De Consecr. Eccl.*, *apud* Rock, *op. cit.*, p. 327.

is *uncut and closed in on all sides*, that it may shew forth the unity and integrity of the true faith."[1] Honorius of Autun (early XIIth century) says: "The chasuble is put over all the other vestments, by which is indicated charity, which is believed to stand higher than all the other virtues. For the chasuble is so called because it is like a little house, and as a man is wholly covered over by a house, so the whole body of the virtues is embraced by and contained in charity."[2] Pope Innocent III (end of XIIth century) who was, incidentally, the founder of our present sequence of liturgical colours, remarks: "Over all the other vestments the priest puts on the chasuble, which signifies charity. For 'Charity covereth a multitude of sins.' . . . The *breadth* of the chasuble signifies the breadth of charity, which is extended even to enemies."[3] Lastly Odericus of Siena (early XIIIth century) adds his indirect testimony to the shape: "By the chasuble which the priest puts on last of all, you must understand charity, . . . *which he lifts up on his arms*, that he may extend it to all by his works of love."[4]

While the period of which we have been speaking may be said to mark the growth of medieval art, so the first half of the XIIIth century may, we think, be justly regarded as marking its climax, and the period from the XIVth to the end of the XVIth may be taken as representing its decline and practical extinction.

The XIIIth century, we repeat, is now almost universally admitted to have marked the culminating point of those centuries which have not inaptly been called the "Ages of Faith." It was indeed no ordinary time that produced such glories of architecture as Amiens, Chartres, Beauvais, the Ste. Chapelle, and, in our own country, Westminster, Wells, Sarum and much of what is finest in our other old cathedrals. We cannot here speak of its illustrious roll of saints, or of the great religious movements which germinated and grew within its bounds, but we should be indeed surprised if the ornaments of the Church and the vestments of her ministers at a time so renowned for faith and piety were anything but worthy of its spirit. Nor indeed are we disappointed, for, though not very many actual

1 *De Divin. Offic.* I, xxii, *apud* Rock, *ibid.*

2 *Gemma Animae*, I, ccvii, *P.L.* CLXXII; or *apud* Rock *ibid.*, and Marriott, *op. cit.*, p. 136.

3 *De Sacro Altaris Mysterio*, I, xlviii, *apud* Rock, *ibid.* or Marriott, p. 155.

4 *Apud* Rock, *ibid.*

vestments of this date have come down to us in their original form, representations in MSS. and stained glass, and effigies on tombs, abound to shew us the dignified and truly splendid nature of the liturgical vestments of this time. Their shape was in general exactly the same as it had been for hundreds of years before, and it is interesting to note that this shape remained substantially the same even in Italy, the cradle of the Renaissance, and in Rome itself, until much later; it is, in fact, that shewn upon sepulchral monuments in the Eternal City and all over Italy right down to the XVIth century. In England, too, the very last brass ever engraved of a Catholic prelate, that of Bp. Purseglove, who died in 1579, shews the bishop in complete pontificals, which, allowing for the difference of technique in the drawing, and of style in the ornament, as far as the general form is concerned are almost identical with those of many centuries before. It is, of course, possible that some allowance should be made when considering these monuments for deliberate archaism of modelling or drawing, but even if this be so it only goes to show how artists in a decadent Age still looked to the earlier forms as to something better and more ideal.

Among the most prominent features of the medieval liturgical wardrobe were the Apparels. These, as we have seen, existed on dalmatics and albs from the earliest times, in the form of bands of enrichment running round the cuffs and hems. Their practical use was to strengthen those parts of the garments most exposed to wear. In the Middle Ages, these apparels were still employed for their practical value, but the one round the hem of the alb had been restricted to two panels, the one in front, and the other behind, to strengthen, and incidentally adorn, the alb where the feet in walking were liable to wear it out: the sides were left to hang in their graceful natural folds. The apparels round the cuffs remained more or less as before; and an extra pair was often added to the breast and back, to complete the symbolisation of the Five Wounds, one of the popular devotions of this time. The amice was assisted in its office of preserving the stole and chasuble from grease by the addition of a rich collar, which matched the other apparels, and fitted into the general mystical scheme, as symbolising the Crown of Thorns. With the way in which the apparelled amice was worn all are familiar from the innumerable effigies of the period, and also from examples of our own day; some may even have been fortunate enough to see it in actual use. Apparelled collars were introduced into the Armenian Church by the influence of the Crusaders, and have remained as an ornament of its celebrating ministers to this day. In Milan apparels both round the neck and on the alb are still worn in conformity with the regulations laid down by St. Charles Borromeo, though here the ones at the bottom of the alb are not attached to it, but are suspended independently from the girdle by ornamental cords. The collar, also, at Milan, has been separated from the amice, and is now put on after the chasuble and secured with cords. In Spain, too, apparels are still not uncommonly worn by the sacred ministers, though here, as at Milan, they are usually put on separately from the alb and amice. In England and Northern Europe, wherever these ornaments have been restored, they generally occupy their original position on the amice and on the alb.

The dalmatic, being by nature only a sort of alb, was regarded as able also to receive the same adornments as the alb. The *clavi* had long taken on the appearance of ordinary orphreys, and between them, back and front, were often inserted the apparels near the hem, and those at the breast. Those at the cuffs already existed. There was, however, no fixed rule for either apparels or *clavi*: both were only accidental and in no way essential to the garment, and were often, like the orphreys on the chasuble, omitted either altogether or in part. The apparels on the alb have now usually degenerated into lace: or perhaps it would be more correct to say, have been swamped by it; those on the dalmatics are still to be found, even in very debased examples, as areas of the ordinary material of the vestment surrounded or defined by "gold" braid.

For the benefit of those in this country who look upon apparels as in some way exclusively Anglican—and there are such people—it is worth noting that they were one of the very few things condemned by the reformers under Edward VI, who ordered all albs to be "*plain*."[1]

In the XIIIth century the material of the vestments was generally a very pliable silk—hand-woven, of course—and often there was no lining, or, if one existed, it was of the lightest material possible, with no thought of artificial stiffening. The orphreys and apparels were of a richer material, often studded

1 Rubric of the 1st Book of Common Prayer (1549)

Brogi] [*Florence*

FIGURE IV.

XIVTH CENTURY PAINTED WOODEN STATUETTE OF SIENESE WORKMANSHIP, NOW IN THE MUSEO NAZIONALE AT FLORENCE.

The detail of the chasuble and mitre, and especially that of the orphreys, is of the type then very popular throughout Italy, and may be seen to be purely Gothic in character. At the same time the disposition of the orphreys follows the usual Italian tradition : T-cross in front, narrow band acting as collar round the neck, and vertical pillar (invisible, of course, in the photograph) at the back. The dalmatic seems to have been painted almost as an afterthought on the surface of the alb, the carver having apparently forgotten to allow for it or for the maniple. In Italian effigies the stole-ends very seldom shew below the dalmatic. The absence of alb or amice apparels is also in accordance with the Italian custom of the time ; the use of the alb apparels does not seem ever to have been widespread except at Milan, and the amice apparel or collar came into fashion later, in the XVth century, and, again except at Milan and in certain other isolated instances, did not outlast the XVIth century. The chasuble shewn here is of a slightly later Gothic type than that of Cardinal Consalvi mentioned in the text (p. 18), but which owing to its position is difficult to reproduce ; it should be compared with the renaissance one of Martin V (frontispiece), which is of much the same size and has exactly the same disposition of orphreys, though the pallium and folds make these somewhat difficult to discern. For shape of these chasubles, see Diagram, Nos. II or IV (Martin V) and III or V (this statuette), and for the disposition of the orphreys Nos. B and C.

Adrian Harding] [*Godalming*

FIGURE V.

The Chasuble, which is shown on an exceptionally tall figure, is in conformity with S. Charles Borromeo's measurements, and is cut to shape No. VII in the Diagram.

Adrian Harding] [*Godalming*

FIGURE VI.
CELEBRANT, DEACON, SUB-DEACCN AND ASSISTANT PRIEST VESTED FOR MASS.
This set of Vestments was used at the solemn opening of Blackfriars, Oxford, in the presence of H. E. Cardinal Bourne, Whit-Monday, 1929.

Figure VII.
Robert de Wadeby, Archbishop of York (✠ 1397). From the Brass in Westminster Abbey.

Very little need be said of this beautiful effigy. The chasuble is clearly very supple and extremely full and almost certainly represents the completely conical form shewn at the head of the Diagram (No. 1).

with jewels, and usually of a different colour from the body of the vestment. The stole and maniple almost universally matched these and not the vestments themselves, both in design and colour. It was at this period too that the proportions of the different vestments reached their highest point of excellence: stoles were long and reached almost to the ground; the maniple was long and graceful; both stole and maniple were narrow and if they spread out at all at the ends it was at most only a very little; dalmatics were long and soft, not like the "cardboard" ones of nowadays, and emphasised the grace and dignity of the human form; the cope was unrivalled for its majestic folds, and its hood sprang from the shoulders, and was not affixed at a point half way down the back, as so often now, but fell back from the neck and covered the narrow orphrey; the alb was of full length and hung in the natural folds of fine linen, untortured by starch and artificial pleats and unspoilt by the effeminacy of lace: relieved only by the rich colours of the apparels, before and behind; and lastly the chasuble, that most sacred of all the vestments, was supreme in its beauty, adapting itself with its full luxurious folds and graceful lines to the wearer's every movement, and lending added dignity and majesty to the priest of God. Such were the vestments which the paintings and statuary of the times show us to have been used, not merely in the greater functions of the cathedrals and important churches, but in every parish church and chapel throughout the length and breadth of civilised Europe, with no exceptions. Such, too, are the vestments of the sculptured effigies of cardinals and popes in Rome: effigies not only of the XIIIth and XIVth centuries, but of the XVth and XVIth too, vestments all ample and flowing in the extreme, and adorned according to date with a wealth of exquisite Gothic or Renaissance ornament, which shew clearly the falseness and unreality of the modern division of vestments, according to shape alone, into "Roman" and "Gothic."

We may as well say here that such a division, if it be possible at all, cannot in practice be based on any essential differences, but can clearly only be accidental, that is, a distinction based on difference in the style of ornamentation. The Gothic genius did not produce a vestment in any way different from an ordinary Roman one—one, that is, in current and traditional use in connexion with the Roman Rite: all it did was to ornament such a Roman vestment in the manner proper to itself. And this it did, during the Gothic centuries, even in Italy and in Rome itself, so that it is quite the normal thing to find the sculptured chasubles of late XIIIth and XIVth century Italian and Roman effigies enriched with pure Gothic detail, which if differing a little in feeling from our northern Gothic (just as do the Italian Gothic churches of the period) is none the less true Gothic for that.

When, a century later, the return was made in Italy to classical inspiration and motifs, the shape of the chasuble and the other vestments was in no wise affected thereby, at least at first, but only the style of decoration upon them changed. Thus the chasuble in which the effigy of Pope Martin V (†1431) is vested upon his tomb in the Confession of the Lateran Basilica is as full as could be wished, and pliable, but ornamented with *Renaissance* detail; that of Cardinal Consalvi (†1298) in St. Mary Major's, not at all or at most a very few inches wider, is decorated in the *Gothic* style.

Hence if the word "Gothic" as applied to a vestment used in the Latin Mass is to have any meaning at all it must simply mean a Roman (or Latin) vestment ornamented in the Gothic style, just as for a church like Westminster Cathedral, one might decorate a similar vestment with "Byzantine" detail, or with "Baroc" for the Oratory. All would be *Roman* vestments, since all are used for the Roman Rite; this "*genus*" may be divided into "*species*" according to decoration. Hence it appears quite clearly that the attempted division of vestments (especially chasubles) into "Roman" and "Gothic" is a halting one and logically unsound; it is like dividing our countrymen into "Englishmen" and "blondes"; the latter are in reality a subdivision of the former. The proposed division into "Roman" and "Gothic" could be justified only by supposing that the Gothic chasuble was some speciality of the Gothic (Mozarabic) Use, but such a postulate would be quite outside the argument. With greater plausibility might it be urged that a Byzantine chasuble could be fairly classed against a Roman one, if by "Byzantine" be meant not merely ornamental detail but the form itself now used in certain Eastern Liturgies; but here, too, it must be remembered that *originally* even these were one and the same—the Latin *paenula* and Greek φαινόλιον—their present marked dissimilarity being due almost entirely to cutting-down and deformation subsequent to the Middle Ages.

It is true that in and after the XVIth century in the West the cutting-down of the chasuble went ahead (as we shall show directly) at a greatly increased pace, but this mutilation proceeded *all over* the Latin Church, and most rapidly perhaps in those countries, like Germany and Flanders, where the Gothic culture lasted longest; indeed to this day of all the debased forms the Italian is the least removed from the original—though even it has departed much too far!—and there is sometimes but little to choose between a really good Italian and a small so-called "Gothic" chasuble or dalmatic.

Hence it is clear that the division of chasubles and other vestments into "Roman" and "Gothic" (a division which is after all of very recent origin) is a wholly erroneous one; it is even more: it is misleading and should be avoided altogether. All vestments in lawful use in countries following the Roman Rite are "Roman," though they may be decorated in accordance with any national or individual taste or standards provided these be worthy. Within the limits of the current rubrics (which, incidentally, for their due fulfilment demand a chasuble of at least Borromean width), legislation and custom, they may be wider or narrower, ampler or more cut-away; let such descriptions, then, as these, which have the merit of truth and logic, be used instead of the meaningless and misleading "Gothic" or . . . "Semi-Gothic"!

The decline in the shape of the liturgical vestments all over Europe began in earnest in the XVth century, when the introduction of velvet and silk brocades and the increasing heaviness of the embroidery rendered the old and very full shapes, easy enough to wear when made of a supple material, now no longer tolerable; and the same hands which had begun to overlay the vestments with stiff and heavy work of various sorts began also to cut and clip away their ample folds. It was not, however, until the later XVIth, or even the early XVIIth century that any extensive changes and innovations became at all general, and if smaller changes previous to this time had not been allowed to pass wholly unchallenged, these later and more radical ones raised a storm of protest.

From now until the XIXth century "Revival of Christian Art," as Pugin was so fond of calling it, the story of the development of sacred vestments is a sad one: "development" seems indeed hardly the word to use. It was to this period, and especially to the XVIIIth century—that nadir of all the Christian centuries—that we owe the bib-like chasuble, truncated stole and maniple, shrunken surplices or cottas, and other similar vestments—all mere caricatures of the traditional forms.

If anything at all is certain, it is that the Church did not initiate the process which resulted in producing these, but rather that she shewed herself on more than one occasion opposed to it; efforts were made to arrest its progress, and in one case at least regulations were framed which laid down, amongst other things, the minimum dimensions allowable for the chasuble. We refer to the legislation of St. Charles Borromeo for his province of Milan, which obtained the formal approval of the Holy See.[1] In his decrees St. Charles ordered that the chasuble was never to be less, though it might always be more, than 54 inches, in our measure, across the widest part—that is to say, 27 inches at each side of the neck; in the saint's own words: "The chasuble (which some call the *phenolium* or *planeta* from its ample breadth) should be a little more than three cubits[2] wide, so that when falling over the shoulders it may be able to make a fold of at least one palm (about nine inches) below each shoulder." This minimum width brings the chasuble, on an average, to a point actually between the elbow and wrist of the wearer. Let it not be forgotten that St. Charles in giving these dimensions did not necessarily lay down the fullest size he considered desirable, but himself suggests that they represent a minimum standard, designed to put a stop as far as possible to the then growing custom of cutting down the size of the chasuble and other vestments in defiance of all tradition, seemliness or reverence. The length of the chasuble was to be such that it reached "nearly to the heels." In the same regulations the use of apparels on all suitable occasions was insisted on, and these, as we have said, are still used in Milan Cathedral. From the testimony of several authors—among them Pope Benedict XIV[3] —it appears that apparels of some sort continued to be worn by Regulars and in the solemn functions of the Papal Chapel until well into the XVIIIth century. The middle of this same century also saw them still in occasional use in France and Germany.

[1] Ed. Van Drival: *S. Caroli Borromaei Instructionum Fabricae Ecclesiasticae et Supellectilis Ecclesiasticae Libri Duo*, Paris, 1855, *passim.*

[2] A cubit is equivalent to about 18 inches.

[3] *De Sacr. Missae Sacrif. Lib.* I, *cap.* vii, No. 7, Ed. Rome 1783, p. 38.

It is interesting further to note that the Roman chasuble in which Pope Boniface VIII had been buried in 1303, and which was found intact in his tomb in 1605, was, according to measurements taken at the time,[1] about 56 inches wide before and behind, and therefore only about two inches wider than the minimum allowed by St. Charles. A chasuble such as that of Pope Boniface when allowed to hang down fully upon the arms would fall upon and perhaps just cover the hands, and would seem to fulfil very perfectly the conditions demanded by the Rubric of the present Roman *Caeremoniale Episcoporum* (lib. II, cap. viii, §19) which runs as follows : " Then the Bishop rises and is vested with the chasuble, *which is arranged on either side upon his arms, and carefully turned back lest it should encumber him.*"

We may note in passing that the Eucharistic vestments required by the Milanese Use—like those of the Dominican and other variants of the Latin Rite—are not peculiar to Milan, but are similar to those employed in the ceremonies of the Roman Use ; and the difference between the measurements of the " Ambrosian " and those of the " Roman " chasuble noted by Gavanti[2] was merely one of current use. In this distinction of Gavanti we have an early sign of the later and even more misleading classification of chasubles as " Roman " or " Gothic." It is noticeable that many are fond of appealing to Gavanti's measurements, which favour the narrow chasuble, as final (even though they are quite ready to disregard them in the case, for example, of the surplice), though Gavanti himself only offers them as being, in his opinion, more suitable, and, no doubt, in his time more common ; while these same persons make small account of St. Charles's regulations, which, though binding only at Milan, nevertheless obtained official sanction at Rome. Any reader of Gavanti will quickly realise that his measurements are entirely based on the contemporary practice with which he was familiar, and, unlike St. Charles's, have no reference to history or tradition.

St. Charles was far from being alone in his attempt to put a stop to the mutilation of the sacred vestments. Bishop du Saussay of Toul, writing towards the end of the XVIIth century, says :[3]

[1] Grimaldi, in Dionigi, *Vatic. Basil. Crypt. Mon.*, p. 129.

[2] *Thesaurus*, Vol. I, Part V, p. 273, ed. Venice 1823.

[3] *Panoplia Sacerdotalis*, Part I, Book VI, p. 128, Paris 1681.

"So cut down is the chasuble . . . that at the sides it hardly covers the shoulders, much less reaches to the elbows; and this cutting-down has been effected without any sort of warrant of the Holy See or ecclesiastical law, but entirely through the private judgment of individuals. . . . Not only have they deformed the priestly garment itself until it bears no further resemblance whatever to its ancient shape, but they have also deprived it of its mystical reason for being the topmost vestment and enveloping, as it hangs down on all sides from the shoulders, all the other vestments and the whole body of the priest. For it is the common teaching of both ancient and modern interpreters of the rites of the Catholic Church[1] that the chasuble is the symbol of Charity, which overtops all the other Virtues and Gifts. A certain relaxation, however, appears to me to be desirable (saving always the judgment of those wiser than myself) in order that the priest may not be burdened with too great a weight nor impeded in the free use of his arms and hands; never, however, such a relaxation as would entail a departure from what is seemly or allow the arms to appear denuded from the shoulders, but rather such as would leave to the chasuble at least some part of its mystical meaning."

This is, in point of fact, the compromise which was achieved by St. Charles, and has been adopted with success by those who have in our own times succeeded in restoring to the chasuble something of its ancient grace and dignity. From a fresco of the Xth century which existed formerly in the Lateran Basilica and a copy of which is described by Cardinal Bona[2] and by Benedict XIV,[3] it seems that this compromise was not wholly unknown even at that early date; the fresco is one of Pope John XII being vested in a chasuble which covered the forearms, but was not so voluminous as to need turning back upon them; it was cut to a point both before and behind.

In this connexion the words of the old Ritual of Rouen[4] (where the full chasuble seems to have flourished down to the time of the French Revolution) are worthy of note:

[1] Cf. the *Pontificale Romanum*. During the ordination of a priest the bishop, when vesting the *Ordinandus* in the chasuble, says: *Accipe vestem sacerdotalem, per quam* CHARITAS *intelligitur*. . . .

[2] *Rer. Liturg.*, *Lib.* I, cap. xxiv, § viii (t. II, p. 237, ed. Sala, Turin, 1749.)

[3] *De Sacr. Missae Sacrif. Lib.* I, *cap.* viii, No. 14 (p. 44, ed. Rome, 1783).

[4] *Rit. Rothomagense Tom.* I, p. 386. *Apud* Rock *op. cit.*, I, p. 338 (Italics ours).

"Let that form of the sacred vestments be adhered to which the institution of our Fathers and the venerable antiquity of the Cathedral Church dictate, to wit, that the chasuble extend to such a width at either side that it may cover *at least* the whole of the arms; and therefore *let it be made of a suitably pliable material*, that it may easily be lifted up by the hem and may not inconvenience the celebrant."

This type of chasuble is clearly the one envisaged in the *Ritus Celebrandi* at the beginning of the present Roman Missal, in which we read (§ VIII, No. 6): " . . . While the celebrant elevates the Host . . . the minister with his left hand raises the edge of the hinder part of the chasuble *lest it should impede the celebrant in the raising of his arms*, and he does the same again during the elevation of the Chalice."

Coming back once more to the mutilation of the chasuble, we find Cardinal Bona[1] remarking that he could discover "no decree either of Pope or Council" authorising the cutting down of this vestment which had taken place. De Vert, a French author of this period, has many hard things to say of the vestment makers "who," as he says:

"Are allowed the liberty of nibbling, clipping, cutting, slashing, shortening, just as the whim may take them, chasubles, dalmatics, tunicles, and other priestly garments or ornaments which serve for the ministry of the altar; in a word, they give these vestments what shape they like, without consulting the bishop, who should, it would seem, have some right to control the shape of these garments."

The chasuble after such treatment, he adds, "covers neither the arms nor the legs of the wearer."

On the Continent, however, even in the XVIIIth century, the full chasuble had not been altogether abandoned. We have already remarked on its continued use at Rouen. Martène, in his *Voyage Liturgique*, published in 1717,[3] describes with joy, not unmixed with sadness at their dwindling number, the fine full chasubles he was shewn in various places, notably in Cistercian houses (wherein this type of chasuble is again in use to-day) and at Beauvais, where, he says, "they shewed us many fine things, but those I valued most were some ancient chasubles, very full (*toutes rondes*), which are now used only on Maundy Thursday

[1] *loc. cit.*
[2] *Explication des Cérémonies de l'Eglise t.* II, preface, p. xiv (Paris 1710).
[3] Tom. I, Part II, pp. 149, 156.

at the blessing of the Holy Oils, and on Holy Saturday." De Moléon,[1] in his description of a similar journey some forty years later, noted that such chasubles—" quite round and all closed in " (*i.e., conical*)—were still in use in the cathedral of Angers, and that new ones were being made on the same model. These were nearly 60 inches wide, long in proportion (that is, like the Milanese chasubles, nearly to the heels), and very little hollowed out for the arms. He also remarks that at Sens the ancient chasuble ascribed to our own St. Thomas of Canterbury, which is still preserved in the treasury of the cathedral, was in his day worn every year upon the festival of the saint, and that the chasubles in use at Rouen were in conformity with the requirements of the Ritual of that place (cited above). From another source[2] we learn that full chasubles were still occasionally used in Paris at Notre Dame, the Charterhouse, the Abbey of St. Denis, and other churches, as well as in the Cathedral of Metz during Advent and Lent, and in some other French cities ; but these were only isolated survivals, though they persisted in some instances right down to the Revolution.

A " Dictionary of Sacred Objects," published by Magri[3] at Venice in the XVIIIth century has the following on the chasuble :

> " Little by little, instead of being turned back at the sides, it was cut away instead, so that it came to resemble no longer a chasuble but rather a monastic scapular. On this point the Greeks deserve much praise, since they have retained the ancient shape " the loss of which by the Latin Church has been a great misfortune, since " in the shape of the ancient chasuble much majesty and many mysteries were contained ; it originally represented, amongs other things, the Unity of the Church, and the Seamless Garment of Christ, and this in its present cut-away condition it manifestly can no longer do."

Enough has been said to shew that the mutilation of the chasuble, and, in a lesser degree, of the dalmatic, stole, maniple, and other vestments, was deplored by many liturgically and artistically minded people, even while it was in progress ; it was regretted and even put a stop to, wherever possible, by ecclesiastics of high rank ; and it was never in any way formally authorised by the Church. It was carried out almost entirely by those professional vestment-makers who, supplanting the monks and

[1] *Voyages Liturgiques de France*, 1757, pp. 80, 95, 378, 411.
[2] Le Brun, *Explicatio Missae*, t. I, p. 26 (note), ed. Venice 1770.
[3] *Hierolexicon*, Venice, 1735, s.v. *Casula*.

nuns and pious persons of the Middle Ages, to whom this work had been a labour of love, were desirous only of making the largest possible profit and therefore—since they charged "per vestment"—of cutting down the amount of material used to an absolute minimum.

It is, indeed, as Rock[1] himself observes, a striking fact that among all those who during the XVIIth and XVIIIth centuries had thought fit to write on the chasuble and its curtailment, not a single one can be found who approves of its mutilation or sees any beauty or seemliness in its dwindled size; indeed these writers can find no milder words to express their opinion of the new-fangled shape than "degenerated" and "deformed." And what Dr. Rock testifies of those who had written before his time, we think we may reiterate of those who have written in more recent years. All these,[2] with one voice, have deplored the debased forms of the sacred vestments and urged a return to their true and traditional shapes.

One other garment besides the chasuble seems to have suffered to an exceptional extent, and this is the surplice, or, less correctly, cotta. All must know what a surplice looked like in medieval times and even down to the XVIIIth century: representations of it are abundant. It reached almost always to within a few inches of the ground and its sleeves were full like the sleeves of a Benedictine cowl; the whole, like the alb, being of fine linen hanging in its natural folds, and free from lace. It was only at a comparatively recent date that it dwindled to its present niggardly proportions, and the measurements of the surplice in Gavanti[3] were those of the full surplice: "The surplice (identified with the cotta by others who give similar measurements) should have sleeves of such a cut that after being gathered up they may reach to the wrist; they should be about 60 inches round the ends." (Martinucci, in the latest edition, says about 36 inches, but others say that when the hands are joined on the breast the sleeves should hang down to the knees). "The

[1] *Op. cit.*, I, p. 340.

[2] cf. especially, Braun, *I Paramenti Sacri*, 1914, pp. 93—110, or: *Handbuch der Paramentik*, Herder, Freiburg im Breisgau, 1912.

[3] *Thesaurus*, Vol. I, Part V, p. 274, ed. Venice 1823. Similar measurements appeared in the older editions of Martinucci, but in the newer ones (*e.g.*, Pustet 1911, Vol. I, p. 102) they are modified slightly, and Gavanti's are said to be old-fashioned. We give them here, nevertheless, as being more descriptive of the traditional form.

neck should be round rather than square, and on no account slit or opened at the front. The body should fall well below the knees, about half way to the feet; it should be very full and about 5½ yards round the hem (Martinucci says 4 yards). In no part should it be ornamented with the elegance of dainty work, and particularly should it not have pretty niceties upon the shoulders." In the older editions of Martinucci appeared a statement concerning the modern surplice or cotta which was so much *ad rem* that we give it here in full: "The surplice, whose form is now manifold, has been reduced to the level of a mere ornament, but care should be taken that neither in its shape nor in its excessive daintiness should it be unseemly. We cannot pretend to be unaware of the fact that the ornamentation of some surplices is far more suitable to the stage or to be exposed for sale in milliners' shops, than to the use of the clergy while engaged in the sacred functions."

There are not wanting those in England who will have none of the full surplice on the alleged grounds that it is an Anglican garment. True it is that the Anglicans have preserved it for us in something resembling its pre-Reformation form, but it existed as a Catholic vestment long before any Reformed Church was so much as thought of, and it still finds an honourable place in many of our churches. It hardly needs to be pointed out that the principle upon which these adversaries of the surplice base their argument would logically deprive the Catholic clergy of all their sacred vestments (even of the fiddleback chasuble and the lace alb) and of the very Roman collar itself, since all these are now used by many clergymen of the Establishment.

The period of the later Renaissance has had little to shew us beyond the mutilation and even destruction, as far as might be possible, of those forms of the sacred vestments which had been dear to the Catholic Church for upwards of a thousand years; and the alterations which had taken place in the shape of the vestments and particularly in that of the chasuble, had carried with them the loss of the usefulness and rich symbolism of their adornment. But to whatever extent the proportions both of

[1] Vol. I, p. 8, footnote, ed. Rome 1879; in the latest editions; *e.g.*, Pustet, 1911, Vol. I, p. 10, footnote, the phraseology of this statement has been somewhat modified—" profane use " being substituted for " the stage and milliners' shops "—and a note inserted recording the fact that the use of lace is permitted.

whole garments and of each of their component parts have been falsified, fundamentally and essentially the vestments have remained the same : the cut-away chasuble is still a garment with a hole for the neck and no sleeves, if it is no longer wide as Charity, all-embracing as Love ; the dalmatic, stiff now, short and inelegant, still retains its characteristic slits at the side, and an apology for the *clavi* and apparels of an earlier date ; the stole and maniple, now fat and stumpy where once they were slim and graceful, are still essentially a stole and maniple ; the lace alb is still furnished with a modicum of white linen, though this is often tortured into artificial pleats or kept as much out of sight as possible.

All this has its importance in shewing that in making a distinction between the so-called " old " or " medieval " forms—that is to say the present-day " full " or " Borromean " forms—on the one hand, and the " modern " or XVIIIth century ones on the other, or, as some would less accurately describe it, between " Gothic " and " Roman," we distinguish, not between two different vestments, but between two varieties of the same—the one restored to something of its original proportion and beauty, the other maimed and almost grotesque—between the traditional and genuinely Roman forms as worn during the celebration of the Sacred Mysteries by every Pope, bishop, and priest of the Latin Church, for the greater part of the Christian era, and what are little more than caricatures of these venerable forms, the productions of a period, on the one hand, of debased art and taste, and, on the other, of commercial rapacity and caprice.

We feel we cannot do better than conclude with the words of Bishop Ullathorne in which he records the beginning in England of the return to the traditional forms of the Sacred Vestments. " I also assisted," he writes in his Autobiography (I, p. 142), " at the opening of the Chapel at New Oscott (in July 1838) at which all the Bishops were present, as well as a hundred priests. On that occasion the *more ample* form of vestments was first introduced in place of the old form derived from France. Pugin . . . superintended the procession of the clergy and declared that it was the greatest day for the Church in England since the Reformation." While we may perhaps consider that our Church has in point of fact experienced even greater moments since the Reformation than this one, from the point of view of Religious Art at least we must admit the absolute truth of Pugin's words. The movement then begun, in spite of all vicissitudes, and thanks in no small measure to the example of the Benedictines—those faithful guardians of Liturgical Art—the Dominicans and many other communities and individuals, has during the ensuing century grown steadily in England and abroad: so much so that vestments of a more traditional and artistically better form have now for a long while been the established custom in many churches both secular and regular. Pius IX, almost at the outset, refused to condemn them, though strongly urged to do so by, amongst others, Mgr. Corazza in a somewhat violent report[1]; on the contrary, where permission was asked to introduce the better forms, he more than once granted it.[2] Pius X, who wished so earnestly that the Public Prayer of the faithful should be "surrounded with beauty" of every sort, and who pointed in his new Code of Canon Law to "the prescriptions of the liturgy, ecclesiastical tradition and the laws of sacred art" as the true foundations and criteria of all the accessories of divine worship,[3] explicitly, though not officially, approved the restored forms of the Sacred Vestments.[4] The present Holy Father in 1925 blessed several sets for use in the Roman Catacombs. In order, however, the better to control and co-ordinate the movement and bring it more effectively within the bounds of church discipline, the Congregation of the Sacred Rites at the beginning of 1926 published a decree[5] reiterating and strengthening Pius IX's letters reserving to the Holy See the right to permit further restorations and to judge of the expediency of any new departures

[1] *Analecta Iuris Pontificii*, Series XXVII, coll. 867—892, 965—1016. *Cfr.* Barbier de Montault, *Le Costume et les Usages ecclésiastiques selon la Tradition romaine*, *T.* II, *ch.* iii, pp. 26, 27.

[2] *E.g.*, to the French Dominicans, the Diocese of Moulins, etc.

[3] C.I.C., can. 1296, § 3.

[4] For instance: Mgr. Swoboda, Domestic Prelate of His Holiness, informed the Eucharistic Congress at Vienna in 1912 that the Holy Father, after referring, in conversation with him, to the chasubles in use at the German *Campo Santo* close to St. Peter's, which are of unmistakably ample form and which he had some time before expressly approved, added "*The vestments of the Mass must once more be made according to this beautiful large form.*" In view of this, the speaker was having such a chasuble made as an offering for the Pope. (From the Official Report of the Congress, S. Norbertus-Druckerei, Vienna. 1912, p. 545). Another ample chasuble (cut as shape No. VII in the Diagram, and reaching to the wrists) was offered to Pius X by the Benedictine nuns of Dourgne (France) and was subsequently presented by him to the Abbey of Subiaco, where together with a dalmatic and tunicle made to match it, it is now used on certain of the greater feasts.

[5] S.R.C., *Decr. Authent.* No. 4398.

from existing custom. This is entirely as it should be, for only so can chaos be avoided—that very chaos whose beginning we observed when treating of the post-Renaissance period—and unity restored and maintained. May we be so bold as to hope that this unity will be one of *time* as well as *place*—a unity with Antiquity as well as throughout the modern world, a unity similar to that already happily achieved with regard to the sacred chant. There the Church, by the mouth of one of her greatest Pastors in modern times, has spoken clearly, and in doing so has also laid down her general policy : " Our Holy Mother Church, to whom is divinely committed the task of drawing the minds of the faithful towards sanctity, has ever made the happiest use of the accessories of the sacred liturgy in the attainment of this noble end. And in this work (lest variety should breed dissension, nay in order rather that that unity may flourish unimpaired which confers at once vigour and comeliness upon the mystical body of Christ) she has ever made it her special business to preserve with untiring care *the traditions of former Ages*, and if at any time these should have become obliterated during the course of centuries, it has always been her endeavour *diligently to seek them out and firmly to restore them*."[1] May we not indeed hope and pray that these words may be, in God's good time, applied also to the very kindred matter of the Sacred Vestments !

Perhaps someone who has read thus far may think that we have claimed an excessive importance for what is after all a matter of very small moment—a mere " accident," to use a Scholastic term, of the Sacred Liturgy. If anyone think this, let him remember that in the section of the Book of Exodus which is devoted to a description of the construction and furnishing of the Tabernacle, one whole chapter[2] is given up to the recording of the detailed instructions which Almighty God Himself saw fit to give concerning the priestly vestments to be worn by those engaged in offering the imperfect sacrifices of the Old Law. What care, then, can be too great, what thought too much, to spend upon those vestures which are to clothe and to adorn the Christian priest and his assistants in the performance of that greatest of all acts, the offering up of the August and Awful Sacrifice of the Lamb ?

[1] Vatican Gradual (1906) ; opening words of the Introduction (Edn. Desclée, p. vii). (*Italics ours*).

[2] Exodus, xxviii.

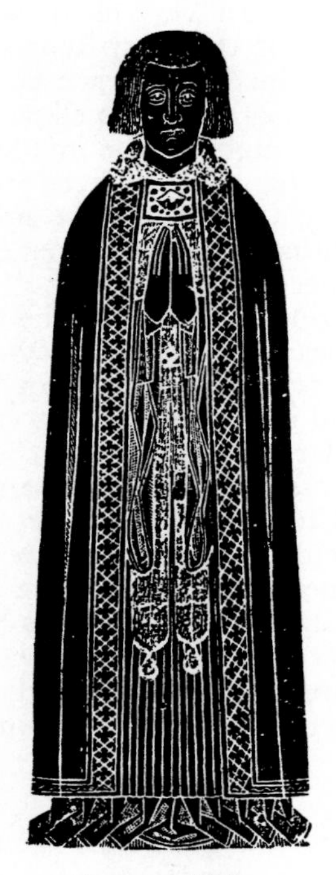

FIGURE VIII.

SILVESTER GABRIEL

(PRIEST, ✠ 1512)

Church of S. John the Baptist, Croydon.

The *Surplice* should be noted with its full sleeves, and body reaching nearly to the ground. The two pendants and small hood or collar belong to the *almuce*, a garment no longer in current use, but bearing some resemblance to the *cappa* or tippet worn by canons and vicars-choral.

Adrian Harding] [*Godalming*

FIGURE IX.

PRIEST IN MASS VESTMENTS.

The chasuble is of a modified bell or conical shape (No. II or IV in the Diagram).

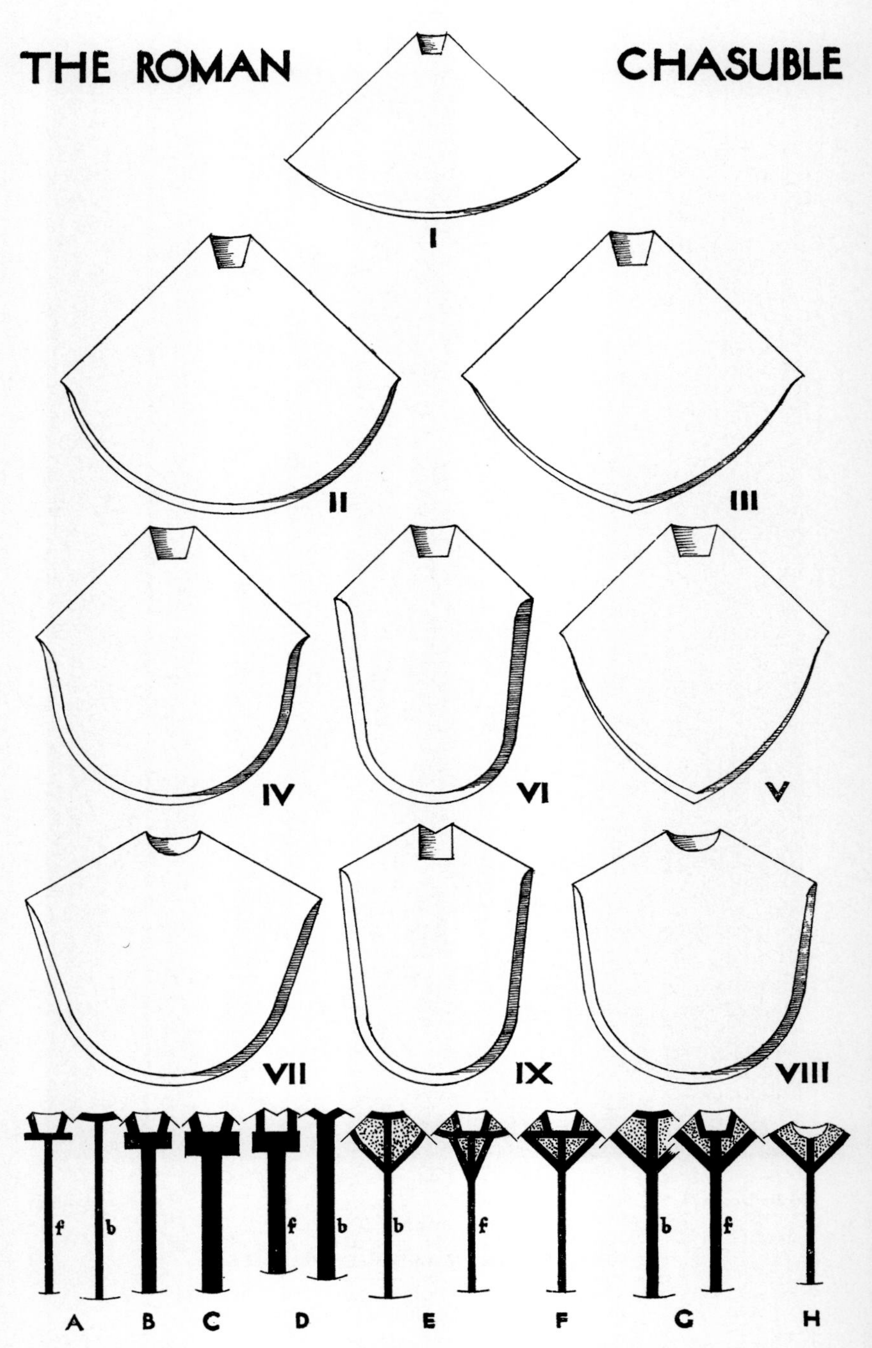

(*Reproduced by kind permission from the Prinknash Benedictines' Catalogue of Sacred Vestments*).

To face page 31.

EXPLANATION OF THE DIAGRAM.

I.—The Original Conical Form (drawn to a slightly smaller scale than the others). This was at first common to both East and West, and remained in general use throughout the West until the XIIIth century at least.

II, III.—XIIIth and XIVth century modifications.

IV, V.—XVth and XVIth forms, still further modified.

VI.—A XVIth century form. This was the final modification of the steep-sided chasuble. Having reached this limit, it was now found possible and in some ways more convenient to raise the angle at the sides to obtain a better fit on the shoulders and round the neck. This being done, we arrive at :

IX.—A XVIth—XVIIth variation of the preceding.

In the XVIIIth and XIXth centuries the same form was used, but progressively smaller, more and more scooped out at the sides in front, and squarer at the bottom.

VIII.—A XIXth century restored form with high sides.

VII.—A XXth century amplification of this form.

When the restoration began in the early XIXth century, the then common form (No. IX) was simply broadened. But at the same time seams were introduced upon the arms (*i.e.* at the sides) which was a serious departure from tradition, for, as stated in the text, the ancient forms always had their seams vertically down the centre of the back and/or front. Sometimes an auxiliary horizontal seam might occur across the front, made necessary by the use of a narrow fabric ; in the narrower forms of chasuble this often came fairly high up, upon the breast, and it was by means of this seam (which still exists, to the exclusion of " shoulder " seams, in the modern Italian chasuble) that the alteration in the angle of the shoulder-line was effected. In restoring the width of the chasuble it is obvious that the ancient position of the seams and the old steep shoulder-line should be revived, for thus only can the same effect of drapery be obtained that we admire so much in ancient monuments and paintings, and thus only will the restoration be a true one.

At the foot of the diagram are shewn representative drawings of orphreys (f=front view ; b=back view). **A** is the earliest ; the disposition explains itself. **B, C, D** shew the same disposition in varying widths ; **D** in particular shews how it has survived until to-day on the Italian chasuble. **E** to **G** shew type **A** complicated by the addition of a Y-cross. The Y-cross seems to have arisen through the addition of an extra thickness or " yoke " to the upper part of the chasuble, over the shoulders. This yoke was sometimes added underneath as a lining (as in an interesting XIIIth century example at Castel S. Elia near Rome), sometimes on top. In Saxon times it became very rich and was known as the " Flower." In the drawings the position occupied by it is dotted. Its edge hardened into the Y-orphreys, which are now often found on their own without the yoke or flower. In all the schemes **A—G** the original square neck is shewn ; **H** shews the orphreys adapted to forms VII and VIII and the round neck which usually goes with them.